The Art of
Paper Piercing

Marianne Perlot

FORTE PUBLISHERS

Content

Fifth printing May 2004
ISBN 90 5877 185 7

This is a publication from
Forte Publishers BV
P.O. Box 1394
3500 BJ UTRECHT
The Netherlands

Publisher: Marianne Perlot
Editor: Hanny Vlaar
Photography and digital image editing: Fotografie Gerhard Witteveen, Apeldoorn, the Netherlands

Preface

Ornare, the art of paper piercing. This new, enjoyable hobby offers something for everyone. And the Ornare piercing templates offer even more possibilities. These templates with attractive piercing patterns can be used time and time again. Furthermore, piercing is wonderful. You never go wrong and it is always attractive.

And those who think that the patterns are always the same are wrong. You can make many different patterns with just one template by, for example, using just a part of the pattern or by making combinations with a small part of the pattern.

This book is full of examples. The cards in each chapter are made using the same template and you can see that you can make most attractive patterns. Some parts of a template's pattern have been printed in the book. Each photograph shows a number of cards that you can make using only these patterns, so you do not have to buy all the templates in order to make these attractive cards.

Marianne

Techniques

Stick the piercing template with the engraved Ornare text on a card using non-permanent adhesive tape. Pierce the pattern. Use a pencil to draw a line around the border of the template.

Remove the adhesive tape and the template, and cut the pattern along the pencil line. The back of the card, where the piercer comes out of the card, is the good side of the pattern.

You must make sure that you keep the piercer vertical. If you hold the piercer at an angle, as you would holding a pen when writing, then the holes are not nice and round, but large and unattractive.

Push the piercer all the way through so that the holes are large and all the same size. It is also possible that the template may move slightly if you are in the middle of piercing and turn the template over to see what it looks like. This will cause a problem, because the non-permanent adhesive tape is not very strong. You can prevent this by securing the corners of the template to the piercing mat using hat pins. This means that you will not be able to see what the patterns look like whilst in the middle of piercing, but it guarantees a perfect pattern. Securing the template in place with pins is very useful for children.

Piercing part of the pattern

If you need part of a pattern, you can see reasonably well where the pattern will come on the card by looking through the holes. If you find it difficult to see, first pierce a hole where you wish to have the pattern and use the hole as a target in your pattern.

Making combinations

If you combine patterns, you can look for a connecting point, or in other words, a point where the patterns touch each other. It is useful to secure such a point using a hat pin, so that you can rotate the template whilst looking at the other side of the pattern to see whether everything falls in place.

Make sure you always work on the back of the card. It has happened to me more than once, that I wanted to look and see how attractive the card is, but then forget to turn the card back over so that I continued piercing on the front of the card.

Piercing straight lines

A lot of straight lines of holes are pierced around a card. First, draw thin lines (on the back of the card where you are going to pierce) using a pencil where the lines of holes will go. Whilst piercing, place your ruler right up against the pencil line. This will help you to keep lines nice and straight. As you get better, you may be able to pierce without first having to draw lines. If you have to pierce close to a border (or on a strip of paper), then the paper may become dented,

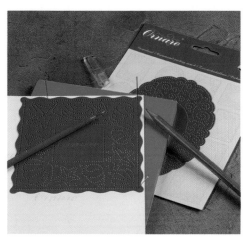

1. Pierce the pattern in the paper.

2. Cut a decorative border.

3. Stick a picture on the part of the card which has not been pierced.

4. Stick it on coloured paper and then on a card.

and this does not look very nice. You can prevent this by placing a piece of scrap paper on the piercing mat under the piercing pattern. The paper may be very thin, but it will still give that little bit of support which is necessary to pierce nice holes.

3D cutting

Most pictures are made using two or three layers. The cutting patterns are not given, because they are very clear. Use the whole picture for the first layer. Next, cut away everything which is in the background. Finally, only cut out the bit of the picture which is in the foreground. Stick the cut out pictures onto each other using pieces of 3D foam tape. If you use two layers, use thick 3D foam tape. If you use more than two layers, use thin 3D foam tape.

Adding glitter

Use a thin brush and white hobby glue to mark the place where the glitter is to be added. Spread the glitter on the wet glue and shake the excess glitter off the card into a piece of paper which has been folded double, so that you can put the excess glitter back in the pot. Allow the glue to dry. There are a lot of nice glitter colours to choose from. You can also use Scribbles.

Remember to always clean the brush thoroughly with water.

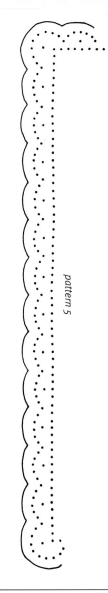

pattern 5

Materials

- Ornare paper piercing templates
- Ornare cutting sheets
- Ornare piercer and piercing mat
- Ornare paper piercing paper (cream)
- Ruler
- Pencil
- 3D scissors
- Photo glue
- Card
- Non-permanent adhesive tape (Scotch Magic Tape)
- Pictures
- 3D foam tape
- Card in matching colours
- Scribbles or glitter

Ornare paper piercing templates
Red templates with a lace-like pattern of holes. You can pierce all the holes or just a part of the pattern.

Ornare piercer and piercing mat
The piercer fits exactly into the holes, and the piercing mat is thick and strong enough to be able to push the piercer into.

Ornare cutting sheets
Attractive pictures (all printed three times so that they are ideal for making 3D pictures) which fit in the empty spaces in the piercing patterns.

Ornare paper piercing paper
Cream paper suitable for piercing attractive, lace-like patterns.

Card, 160 grams Canson (mi-teintes)
Strong paper for folding cards and for using as a background for the pattern which has been pierced.

Romantic flowers

Romantic bouquets of flowers that go well with the lace-like pierced borders.

What you need
- ❏ *Ornare leaves piercing template (PR0504)*
- ❏ *Pictures with flowers*
- ❏ *Scribbles or glitter*
- ❏ *Figure border scissors*
- ❏ *Ornare paper piercing paper*

The Good Luck card and the square card are made using patterns 1 and 2.

Card with mice (see front cover)

The picture used for this card is on a poster sheet (50 x 70 cm) from the Medici Society. This sheet contains 8 different oval pictures which are printed 5 or 6 times.

Standing card with a circle (1)

Pierce the template's pattern in Ornare paper piercing paper and cut it out using figure scissors. On the inside of the pierced circle, cut out a circle (Ø 6.5 cm)

approximately 2 mm from the holes. Stick a picture partially behind the card and leave a piece over the pattern. Stick it all on dark green card (10 x 14.5 cm) and then stick this on soft green card (10.5 x 15 cm). Make the rose 3D and stick everything on a blue double card (12 x 16.5 cm).

Standing card with an oval (2)

Pierce pattern 1 (not the innermost oval) in soft green card and cut it out.

Stick a picture on it, which has been cut out to the size of the innermost oval. Stick the green oval on top of the template (over the circle) using non-permanent adhesive tape. Pierce what you can still see of the pattern in cream card. Cut along the border using figure border scissors and stick this on blue card (10.3 x 14.7 cm). Make the rose and the small white flowers 3D and stick everything on a soft green double card (11 x 15.5 cm).

Square card (3)

Pierce the top part of pattern 2 in opposite corners of a square cream card (9.5 x 9.5 cm). Pierce a line of holes around the card. Take a 4.5 cm wide strip of soft green card and cut this to a size that fits inside the pierced square. Place the strip under the square and pierce the holes of the square through it.

Next, cut the strip on the inside of the holes.

Pierce a line of holes at the top and bottom. Make the flowers 3D and stick everything on a square dark green card (11 x 11 cm) which has been cut to size using figure border scissors. Stick this on a blue double card (12 x 12 cm).

Get well soon (4)

Take a soft green rectangle (7 x 10.5 cm) and pierce a line of holes around it. Stick this on top of the template (over the circle) using non-permanent adhesive tape and pierce what you can still see of the pattern in cream card. Cut the border using figure border scissors and stick this on dark green card (10.3 x 14.6 cm). Make the flower 3D and stick everything on a blue double card (10.5 x 14.7 cm). Only have the bottom and the right-hand side of this card visible.

Good luck (5)

Pierce pattern 1 in soft green card and cut it out. Pierce a line of holes around the border of a blue rectangle (5.7 x 7.5 cm). Pierce a border along a cream rectangle (8 x 12 cm) which has been cut out using figure border scissors.
Pierce pattern 2 in the middle of the card. Make the flower 3D and stick everything on a dark green card (9.5 x 13 cm) and then stick this on a soft green double card (10.5 x 14.7 cm).

Birds

These friendly birds are suitable for making greetings cards for any occasion.

What you need
- ❏ *Ornare flower piercing template (PR0509)*
- ❏ *Ornare birds cutting sheet (OK003)*
- ❏ *3D cutting sheet (3D360)*

The card with the crested tit is made using patterns 3, 4 and 5.

Card with redstart (1)

Pierce the template's pattern in pastel green card and cut it out. Stick this on dark green card (10.4 x 14.4 cm) and then stick this on a soft orange double card (11 x 15.5 cm). Make the bird 3D and stick this on the card.

Landscape card with crested tit (2)

Pierce the inner rectangle (arches, pattern 3) in soft orange card. Cut it out and stick it on a dark green rectangle (6.2 x 7.5 cm). Pierce the outer rectangle with arches (using, for example, pattern 5) in pastel green card (10.2 x 14.4 cm). Cut it out and pierce two daisies in the top right-hand corner (pattern 4). Make the bird 3D and stick everything onto a soft orange double card (10.5 x 14.7 cm).

Standing card with king fisher (3)

Pierce a line of holes around a rectangular soft orange card (5.2 x 6.2 cm). On green card (8.5 x 13.2 cm), pierce the flowers in the corners and on the long sides and connect them with a line of holes. Take the soft orange rectangle, place it on the back of the green card and draw around it using a pencil. Pierce half flowers on the top and bottom of this and pierce holes around the rest of the rectangle just outside the pencil line. Stick this on a soft orange rectangle (9.5 x 14 cm) and pierce holes around the border. Make the bird 3D and stick everything onto a dark green double card (10.5 x 14.7 cm).

Get well soon (4)

Pierce the largest part (see the photograph) of the short side of the template twice in pastel green card and cut the patterns out. Stick these on dark green card (3.8 x 9.3 cm). Stick this on green card (9.7 x 14 cm) and pierce holes around the border. Make the two roses 3D with one layer (cut them out leaving a border around them). Stick everything onto a soft orange double card (10.5 x 14.7 cm) and pierce holes around the border.

Label (5)

Pierce the inner arch of the rectangle (pattern 3) in pastel green card. Cut this out and round off the corners. Pierce a flower in one of the corners. Stick this on green card (6.8 x 8 cm) and round off the corners. Make the rose 3D with one layer and stick everything onto a dark green double card (7.6 x 9 cm).

pattern 2

pattern 1

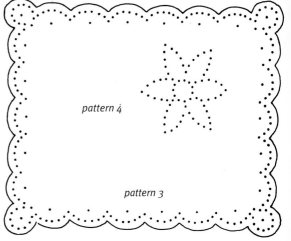

pattern 4

pattern 3

1.

4.

5.

3.

2.

Marriage

Lovely romantic rose cards for festive congratulations.

What you need

❑ Ornare dove piercing template (PR0502)
❑ Ornare marriage cutting sheet (OK007)
❑ 3D cutting sheet (3D360)

The card with the wedding car and the lovebird are made using patterns 6, 7 and 8.

Bridal sweet (1)

Pierce the template's pattern in pastel pink card. Cut it out and stick in on burgundy card (12 x 12 cm). Make the bridal sweet 3D and stick everything on an old rose double card (12.5 x 12.5 cm).

Homing pigeon (2)

Take a strip of pastel pink card (3 x 15 cm) and pierce the heart with the curls three times in full in the middle and half of the pattern on the sides. Start with the middle heart exactly in the middle and have the outer pierce of the curls join together. Stick this on burgundy card (3.5 x 15 cm).

Stick a strip of old rose card underneath on the sides. Pierce arches in it and cut it out. Stick everything on a pastel pink card (10.5 x 14.7 cm).

Wedding car (3)

Pierce the inner square (pattern 7) in pastel pink card (5.1 x 5.1 cm) and round off the corners. Stick this on burgundy card (6 x 6 cm) and round off the corners. Take a piece of old rose card (8 x 12 cm) and round off the corners. Place the burgundy square on the back and draw around it using a pencil. Next, pierce holes all the way around just outside this line. Do the same with the pink rectangle on a pastel pink double card (10.5 14.7 cm). Pierce a hole in the pink rectangle 1.7 cm under the middle of the pierced square and let this be the connecting point for the two doves. Pierce the doves (pattern 6). Make the wedding car 3D and stick all the separate bits of the card on top of each other.

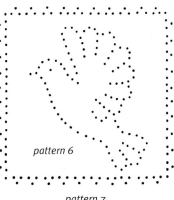

pattern 6

pattern 7

Lovebird (4)

Take a pastel pink rectangle (6 x 12 cm). Pierce a line of holes around the border and pierce a small square in the middle (pattern 7). Pierce a dove (pattern 6) on both sides. Let the beak join the square's fifth outer pierce from the top. Stick this on burgundy card (6.5 x 12.5 cm). Pierce the arch border (pattern 8) in pastel pink card (8 x 14 cm) and cut it out. Start at the corners and pierce six arches along the top and bottom, and three arches along the sides. Make the lovebird 3D and stick everything on a pastel pink double card (10.5 x 14.7 cm) and pierce a line of holes around the border.

Wedding bells (5)

Take an old rose square card (8.5 x 8.5 cm) and draw the outline of the 3D picture on the back. Pierce a hole in each corner just outside the pencil line as well a hole exactly in the middle of each side, also just outside the pencil line. Have these holes join the bottom hole of the hearts which you are going to pierce. Pierce a small heart with curls on the sides (leave out the bottom curls) and pierce a big heart without any curls in each corner. Pierce a line of holes around the border of the square. Pierce the arch border in pastel pink card (10 x 10 cm). Cut it out and stick it on burgundy card (10.2 x 10.2 cm).

Make the wedding bells 3D and stick everything together on a pastel pink double card (11.2 x 11.2 cm).

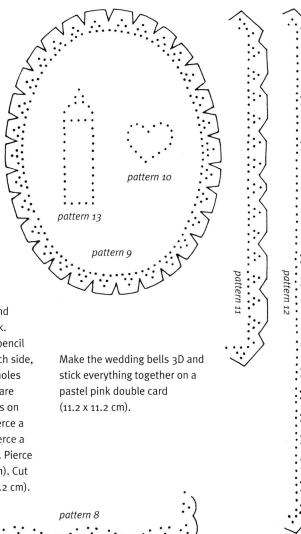

pattern 10

pattern 13

pattern 9

pattern 11

pattern 12

pattern 8

Birth

The blue cards are for a baby boy. You can also chose to use pink paper or another colour that goes well with the colour the parents have chosen for the nursery.

What you need
- ❏ *Ornare baby piercing template (PR0511)*
- ❏ *Ornare baby cutting sheet (OK004)*
- ❏ *3D cutting sheet (3D360)*

The cards with the stork and the bear, as well as the label with the stork, are made with patterns 9, 10, 11, 12 and 13.

On the scales (1)

Pierce the template's pattern in pastel blue card. Cut it out and stick it on dark blue card (9.8 x 14.2 cm). Next, stick this on a blue double card (10.5 x 15.3 cm) and pierce holes around the border.

Sleeping with a bear (2)

Pierce a line of holes around the border of pastel blue card (8 x 12.5 cm). Pierce an oval on one side (pattern 9) and three bottles (pattern 13) and two hearts (pattern 10) on the other. Pierce a hole as a starting point, for example, on the bottom left-hand side of the bottle and the bottom hole of the heart. Pierce the template's decorative border in blue card (9.5 x 14 cm) (pattern 11). Make the baby and the bear 3D and stick everything, at an angle, on a dark blue double card (10.5 x 14.7 cm).

Stork (3)

Pierce the oval (pattern 9) in pastel blue card and cut it out (only with the template: pierce the shape first, cut it out to a bigger size and then cut out the corners). Stick this on a dark blue square (8.3 x 8.3 cm). Pierce a line of holes around the border and pierce a heart in each corner (pattern 10). Pierce the template's decorative border (pattern 11) in a blue square (9.5 x 9.5 cm) starting from the corners and cut it out. Make the baby and the stork 3D. Stick everything on a pastel blue double card (12.4 x 12.4 cm) and pierce a line of holes around the border.

Socks (4)

Take a strip of pastel blue card (4.8 x 15 cm) and pierce the socks on the top of the template in the middle of the card. Next, pierce the socks pointing in one direction and look for a connecting point (see photograph). Pierce a line of holes at the top and bottom of the strip. Pierce the decorative border on two strips of blue card which are 15 cm long and cut them out.

Stick them behind the pastel blue strip on dark blue card (7 x 15 cm) and then on a blue double card (10.5 x 14.8 cm). Tie a bow of raffia to the card.

Label with a stork (5)

Pierce an oval (pattern 9) in pastel blue card (6.5 x 8.5 cm) and round off the corners. Pierce a heart in each corner (pattern 10). Stick this on blue card (7 x 9 cm) with rounded off corners and then on a dark blue double card (7.5 x 9.5 cm). Make the stork 3D.

Label with a bow (6)

Pierce the decorative border in pastel blue card (6.9 x 9.6 cm) starting from the corners and cut it out. Pierce the socks in one corner.
Stick this on dark blue card (6.9 x 9.6 cm). Cut the corners off and stick this on a blue double card (7.2 x 10.2 cm).
Stick the duck in the top left-hand corner. Make a hole in the ring with a perforator and thread a piece of raffia through it.

Shells

These attractive shell cards are suitable for all occasions.

What you need
❑ *Ornare shell piercing template (PR0500)*
❑ *Ornare shell cutting sheet (OK002)*

The card with the different sections can be made using patterns 14 and 15.

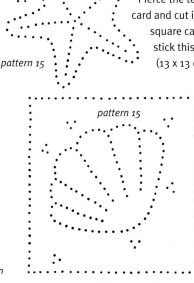

pattern 15

pattern 15

pattern 14

Large square card (1)

Pierce the template's pattern in cream card and cut it out. Stick this on a dark blue square card (12.3 x 12.3 cm) and then stick this on a soft orange double card (13 x 13 cm). Stick a red-brown triangle (long side 3 cm) in each corner and keep the edge of the card free.

Standing card (3)

Pierce the 3 figures on the left-hand side of the template on a strip of cream card (3 x 15 cm). Pierce the starfish in the middle of the strip and pierce the 2 shells on both sides of it. Stick this on dark blue card (3.5 x 15 cm). Pierce the small starfish on two cream triangles (long side 3.5 cm) and stick these on dark blue triangles (long side 4 cm). Pierce the small square on red-brown card (5x 5 cm). Make the shells 3D and stick everything on a soft orange card (10.5 x 14.7 cm).

Standing card (2)

Pierce the inner square on red-brown card (5 x 5 cm). Pierce the template's smallest starfish in each corner of a soft orange square card (8 x 8 cm) and pierce a line of holes around the border. Pierce the template's 3 figures in the bottom left-hand corner on cream paper (9.3 x 13.7 cm) and pierce a line of holes around the border. Make the picture 3D and stick everything on a dark blue double card (10.5 x 14.7 cm).

Square card with different sections (4)

Pierce the small square (pattern 14) twice in red-brown card (5 x 5 cm) and twice in soft orange card (5 x 5 cm). Pierce the largest shell (pattern 15) in one of the soft orange squares and the largest starfish (pattern 15) in the other. Also pierce a couple of triangles using three holes. Stick these squares on dark blue card (5.2 x 5.2 cm). Pierce the template's large square in a cream square card (11.5 x 11.5 cm) or pierce your own line of holes around the border. Divide the back of the pierced square into 4 equal sections using a pencil and pierce lines of holes along the pencil lines.
Make the shells 3D and stick everything on a dark blue double card (12.5 x 12.5 cm).

Party

Presents, champagne and flowers

for a special, festive occasion!

What you need
❏ Ornare party piercing template (PR0510)
❏ Ornare party cutting sheet (OK008)
❏ 3D cutting sheet (3D360)

The cards with the champagne bottle and the presents can be made using patterns 16, 17 and 18.

Flowers (1)

Pierce the template's pattern in soft yellow card. Cut it out and stick in on dark green card (9.5 x 14 cm). Cut 4 triangles (short sides 4.5 cm) out of yellow marbled card and stick these in the corners of a brick red double card (10.5 x 14.7 cm) and keep an edge of the card free. Make the bunch of flowers 3D.

Congratulations (2)

Take a strip of yellow marbled card (3.5 x 11 cm). Pierce a line of holes along the top and bottom and pierce the party hat a number of times at the same angle. Stick this on dark green card (4 x 11 cm). Pierce the streamer on the left-hand side of the template twice in soft yellow card (8.3 x 12.8 cm) and pierce a line of holes around the border. Stick this on brick

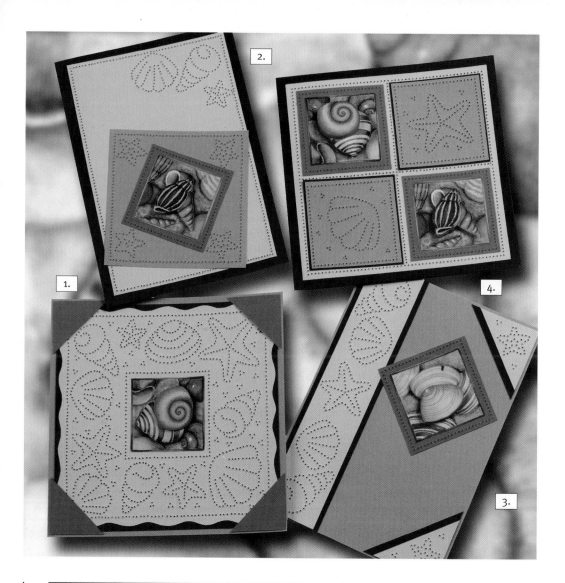

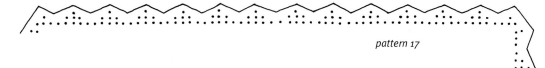

pattern 17

red card (9.5 x 14 cm) and pierce the template's decorative border around the edge. Make the champagne glasses 3D and stick everything on a dark green double card (10.5 x 14.7 cm). Cut the strip to the size of the card.

Champagne bottle (3)
Pierce the template's decorative border (pattern 17) in yellow marbled card (long sides 12 points, short side 7 points) and cut it out. Pierce the rectangle (at an angle) on the left-hand side of the card and pierce two balloons on the right-hand side of the card (pattern 16). Stick this on brick red card (10 x 14.3 cm) and pierce a line of holes around the border. Make the champagne bottle 3D and stick everything, at an angle, on a dark green double card (10.5 x 14.7 cm).

Presents (4)
Pierce the small rectangle (pattern 18) on brick red card (5.4 x 6.8 cm). Pierce the decorative border (pattern 17) on yellow marbled card (8 x 9.5 cm) and cut it out with 6 points along the top and bottom and 7 points on the sides.
Stick this on dark green card (9 x 10.5 cm) and pierce a line of holes around the border. Make the presents 3D. Stick everything on a soft yellow double card (10.5 x 14.7 cm) and pierce a line of holes around the border.

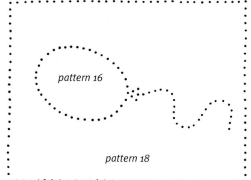

pattern 16

pattern 18

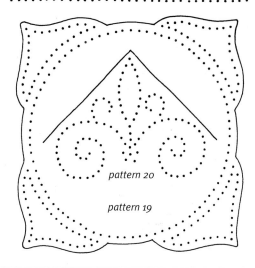

pattern 20

pattern 19

Valentine's and Mother's Day

Romantic greetings for special friends (which you don't need to only send on February 14) and your mother.

What you need
- ❏ *Ornare baroque piercing template (PR0501)*
- ❏ *Valentine 3D cutting sheet (AV9333)*

The cards with the bear and the angel can be made using patterns 19 and 20.

I love you (1)

Pierce a part of the template (see the photograph) in cream card (9.5 x 9.5 cm) and stick this on brick red card (10 x 10 cm). Make the rabbit and the hearts 3D, and stick everything on a burgundy double card (10.5 x 14.7 cm). Stick some hearts and the text in the circle.

Love and kisses (2)

Stick a strip of cream card (7.2 x 15.5 cm) diagonally on the piercing template using non-permanent adhesive tape. Pierce two opposite corners and cut them out. Stick this on burgundy card and cut this out with a small border. Pierce the circle in light brown card and cut it out. Make the doves 3D. Stick everything on a brick red double card (10.5 x 14.7 cm) and pierce a line of holes around the border.

Box of chocolates

Pierce the template's pattern in cream card. Cut it out and stick it on a square burgundy card (11.5 x 11.5 cm). Cut 4 triangles out of light brown card (long side 3 cm) and stick them in the corners of a brick red square card (12.5 x 12.5 cm), with a small border visible. Make the box of chocolates 3D and stick everything on the card.

Bear (4)

Pierce pattern 19 in cream card. Cut it out and stick it on a square burgundy card (6.5 x 6.5 cm). Stick this on a square brick red card (7.3 x 7.3 cm) and pierce a line of holes around the border. Pierce pattern 20 in the four corners of a light brown double card (10.5 x 14.7 cm). Make the bear 3D and stick everything on the card.

Angel (5)

Pierce pattern 20 in the four corners of a square light brown card (11.5 x 11.5 cm). Pierce only the curls of the pattern in the area between the corners along the

edges. Make the angel 3D. Stick this with some hearts on a square cream card (6.2 x 6.2 cm) and pierce a line of holes around the border. Stick this on a brick red square card (7.5 x 7.5 cm). Stick everything together on a burgundy square double card (12.5 x 12.5 cm) and pierce a line of holes around the border.

Music and flowers

With a little bit of white hobby glue, you can turn a simple picture into a festive picture which perfectly matches the pierced flowers on the cards.

What you need
- ❏ *Ornare lily piercing template (PR0508)*
- ❏ *Pictures*
- ❏ *Gold glitter/ Scribbles*

The square card can be made using patterns 21 and 22.

pattern 21

Flowers on a landscape rectangle (1)
Pierce the template's pattern in light brown card and cut it out. Stick it on a dark green rectangle (8.8 x 13.1 cm) and pierce a line of holes around the border. Stick this on a cream rectangle (9.5 x 14 cm) and then on a brick red double card (10.5 x 14.7 cm).

Violin (2)
Stick a strip of cream card (5.5 x 14 cm) at an angle on the piercing template using non-permanent adhesive tape and stick the piercing template on light brown card (the template is, therefore, placed between the two pieces of card). Pierce everything on both sides of the cream strip in the light brown card and draw a pencil line around it. Take everything apart. Pierce a line of holes along the long sides of the strip and stick the strip in the empty area of the light brown card. Cut the excess card away. Decorate the picture with Scribbles and stick it on the strip. Stick everything on a dark green double card (10.5 x 14.7 cm) and pierce a line of holes around the border.

Harp (3)

Pierce the template's pattern, except the outer line around the border, in cream card (9.5 x 13 cm). Cut the oval out approximately 2 mm from the holes. Stick the harp through the opening and stick it to the back using adhesive tape. Stick everything on a dark green rectangle (10 x 14 cm) and then on a light brown double card (10.5 x 14.7 cm).

Banjo (4)

Stick a strip of cream card (6 x 14.7 cm) on the template from the top left-hand corner to the bottom right-hand corner and pierce as much of the pattern as possible. Stick this strip on a strip of light brown card (6.8 x 14.7 cm). Next, stick this on a brick red double card (10.5 x 14.7) and pierce a line of holes around the border. Decorate the banjo with Scribbles and stick it on the card.

pattern 22

Flowers on a square (5)

Cut a square (6 x 6 cm) out of light brown card and pierce a line of holes around the border. Stick this on a dark green square card (6.5 x 6.5 cm). Pierce a line of holes around the border of a cream square card (11.5 x 11.5 cm). Place the dark green square card in the middle of the back of the cream card. Draw a pencil line around it and pierce a line of holes approximately 2 mm on the outside of this line. Pierce pattern 21 in the four corners and pierce pattern 22 on the sides. Point all the flowers in the same direction. Stick everything on a square brick red double card (12.5 x 12.5 cm).

Dogs and cats

pattern 23

For all animal lovers who have a preference for dogs and cats!

What you need
- ❏ Ornare curl piercing template (PR0507)
- ❏ Ornare dogs cutting sheet (OK005) and cats cutting sheet (OK006)

The landscape card and the square card can be made using patterns 23, 24 and 25.

Standing card with a sitting cat (1)

Pierce the template's pattern in cream card. Cut it out and stick it on a strip of blue card and a strip of orange card (each card 5 x 14.2 cm). Stick these strips to each other using adhesive tape on the back and then pierce a line of holes around the border. Make the cat 3D and

stick everything on a soft orange double card (10.5 x 14.7 cm).

Standing card with a Yorkshire Terrier (2)
Only pierce the pattern's four curl combinations (do not move the template) in cream card (9.5 x 13.5 cm) and pierce a line of holes around the border. Stick this on dark brown card (10 x 14 cm) and then on a blue double card (10.5 x 14.7 cm). Make the dog 3D and stick it in the middle.

Standing card with a white cat (3)

Pierce holes around the border of a blue rectangle (5.7 x 7.5 cm). Place this on the back in the middle of a cream rectangle (9.7 x 13.3 cm) and draw around it using a pencil. Also draw pencil lines along the diagonals and through the middle of the long and short sides. The border of the card is now divided into eight sections. Pierce a part of the curl combination in each section, starting with the top and bottom (see the photograph). Stick this on dark brown card (10 x 13.6 cm) and then on an orange double card (10.5 x 14.7 cm). Make the cat 3D.

Square card (4)

Cut a square (6 x 6 cm) out of soft orange card. Place this in the middle on the back of a square cream card (10 x 10 cm) with holes pierced around the border. Draw around the square using a pencil and pierce holes

around it just on the outside of the line. Pierce pattern 23 in every corner. Use the holes in the corner as a connection point and stick the cream card on a blue square card (10.5 x 10.5 cm). Stick four triangles (short sides 4.5 cm) on a square orange double card (12.3 x 12.3 cm) and leave a small border. Make the dog 3D and stick everything together.

Landscape card (5)

On a strip of cream card (2.5 x 14.7 cm), draw a pencil line on the back in the middle along its length. Pierce pattern 25 on this with the middle line of holes on the pencil line. Pierce one hole extra on the pencil line and use this as a connecting point with another pierced copy of pattern 25. Pierce the whole strip and stick it on dark brown card (3 x 14.7 cm). Do the same with two strips of orange card (2 x 14.7 cm), except only pierce the line of holes and the curls on one side. Stick these strips under the dark brown card and stick this on a blue card (5.5 x 14.7 cm). Make the cat 3D, pierce pattern 24 in the blue card and stick everything on a cream double card (10.5 x 14.7 cm).

pattern 25

pattern 24

Flowers

Attractive cards with a decorative pierced border and flowers.

What you need
- ❏ *Ornare flower piercing template (PR0506)*
- ❏ *Ornare flower cutting sheet (OK001)*
- ❏ *Valentine 3D cutting sheet (AV9333)*
- ❏ *Glitter*

The square card, the standing card with the soft pink flowers and the label can be made using patterns 26, 27, 28 and 29.

Grape hyacinths (1)

Pierce the template's pattern in pastel pink card. Cut it out and stick it on an old rose card (8.5 x 13.8 cm) with a line of holes pierced in the corners. Stick this on soft green card (9 x 14.5 cm). Make the grape hyacinths 3D and stick everything on a burgundy double card (10.5 x 14.7 cm).

Purple flowers (2)

Stick a strip of cream card (5 x 14.5 cm) over the length of the template using non-permanent adhesive tape and pierce the flower and the stem on the top and bottom. Cut the excess card away according to the template. Stick the strip on a strip of burgundy card (6 x 14.7 cm) and pierce a line of holes on both sides. Pierce pattern 27 in soft green card and cut it out. Make the flowers 3D and stick everything on an old rose double card (10.5 x 14.7 cm).

Landscape card with roses (3)

Only pierce the stems of the template's pattern (do not move the template) in pastel pink card (8.8 x 10.7 cm). Pierce two small leaves (from pattern 29) in the empty space. Round off the corners, and stick this on a burgundy card (9.5 x 14 cm) with rounded off corners and a line of holes pierced around the border. Make the roses 3D and stick everything on an old rose double card (10.5 x 14.7 cm) with rounded off corners.

Standing card with soft pink flowers (4)

Pierce pattern 28 in the middle of pastel pink card (9.5 x 11 cm). Use the outer points of this as connecting points and pierce pattern 26 at the top and bottom and on the left-hand and right-hand sides. Pierce the two small leaves from pattern 29 in the remaining four points. Cut the corners of the card

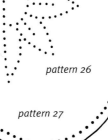

pattern 26

pattern 27

off, from one flower to the next, and stick this on burgundy card (9.5 x 11 cm). Stick a strip of soft green card in which a line of holes has been pierced in the corners. Make the flowers 3D and stick everything on an old rose double card. Pierce a line of holes around the border.

Square card (5)

Pierce a line of holes around a square pastel pink card (10 x 10 cm). First, pierce pattern 29 in every corner and then pierce it again on the sides (a total of eight times). Use holes in the lines as connecting points. Stick this on a square burgundy card (10.5 x 10.5 cm) and then on a square soft green double card (12.3 x 12.3 cm) and pierce a line of holes around the border.

pattern 29

pattern 28

Label (6)

Pierce pattern 26 on the short side of a pastel pink card (5.5 x 9 cm) and cut the excess card away. Pierce a line of holes around the border and stick it on a soft green card (5.8 x 9.5 cm). Round off one side and stick this on a burgundy double card (6.2 x 10 cm).

Shopkeerpers can order the material from:

Avec, Waalwijk, the Netherlands (including Ornare)
Kars, Ochten, the Netherlands (including Scribbles and the pictures shown in this book)

Both shopkeepers and card makers can order poster sheets from Atelier Barbestyn, Kadoelerweg 15b, 8317 PH Kraggenburg, the Netherlands.